SCRIPT: **CHRISTOPHER YOST & ERICT PEARSON**
WRITER: **ERIC PEARSON**
PENCILS: **WELLINGTON ALVES, DANIEL HDR, AGUSTIN PADILLA, LUKE ROSS**
INKS: **DON HO, RICK KETCHAM, MARK PENNINGTON, LUKE ROSS**
COLOURIST: **CHRIS SOTOMAYOR**

LETTERING: **ASTARTE DESIGN, STUDIO RAM**

EDITORIAL TEAM USA
SANA AMANAT, MARK D. BEAZLEY, JENNIFER GRÜNWALD, JON MOISAN,
NELSON RIBEIRO, ALEX STARBUCK, JEFF YOUNGQUIST

C. B. CEBULSKI
EDITOR IN CHIEF

JOE QUESADA
CHIEF CREATIVE OFFICER

DAN BUCKLEY
PUBLISHER

ALAN FINE
PRESIDENT

MARVEL STUDIOS
CREATIVE MANAGER: **WILL CORONA PILGRIM**
DIRECTOR OF DEVELOPMENT: **BRAD WINDERBAUM**
CREATIVE EXECUTIVE: **JONATHAN SCHWARTZ**
SVP PRODUCTION & DEVELOPMENT: **JEREMY LATCHAM**
PRESIDENT: **KEVIN FIEGE**

MARVEL

AVENGERS

This book traces the story of the **Avengers**, Earth's Mightiest Heroes! In the comic books, the original incarnation of Marvel's most important super-hero team came together in 1963. For this, **Stan Lee** and **Jack Kirby** assembled several heroes who had already appeared in comics – **Iron Man**, **Thor**, **Ant-Man**, **Wasp** and the **Hulk** – and over the years, the team's line-up changed many times. Marvel Studios' 2008 box-office sensation Iron Man marked the beginning of a new era of movie success, starring **Robert Downey Jr**. as the high-tech visionary and hero, thrilling fans and critics alike. The appearance of **Samuel L. Jackson** as S.H.I.E.L.D.'s top spy **Nick Fury** in a post-credits scene gave fans hope that something bigger was in the pipeline. Sure enough more movies followed, starring not only Iron Man but also the Hulk, AKA **Dr. Bruce Banner**, **Captain America** and **Thor**, as well as introducing the devious **Loki**, S.H.I.E.L.D. spy **Natasha 'Black Widow' Romanoff** and **Hawkeye**, AKA **Clint Barton**, to the Marvel Cinematic Universe. In 2012, director **Joss Whedon** brought all these characters together in *Marvel Studios' Avengers*, a big-screen spectacular that changed modern cinema and the super-hero genre for ever. Inspired by this success, the TV series *Marvel's Agents of S.H.I.E.L.D.* began in 2013, following the adventures of the spy agency and **Agent Coulson**, a character who made his debut not in a comic book, but in the *Iron Man* movie. Featured in this book is an official comic-book prequel to the movies, focusing on the role of S.H.I.E.L.D. and Nick Fury as they struggle to come to terms with a world in turmoil, full of super heroes, monsters and alien gods! Writers **Eric Pearson** and **Christopher Yost**, who have developed several ideas for Marvel's film and TV universe, pull together the events that lead into Marvel Studios' *Avengers*...

MARVEL MOVIE COLLECTION: MARVEL'S THE AVENGERS MARVEL MOVIE COLLECTION: SPIDER-MAN – HOMECOMING published by **PANINI COMICS**, a division of **PANINI UK Ltd**. Mike Riddell, Managing Director. Alan O'Keefe, Managing Editor. Mark Irvine, Production Manager. Simon Frith, Senior Editor. Office of publication: Brockbourne House, 77 Mount Ephraim, Tunbridge Wells, Kent, TN48BS. Lettering **Astarte Design**, **Fabio Ciacci**, **Elleti**, **Studio RAM**, Chief Executive Officer: Aldo H. Sallustro. Publishing Director Europe: Marco M. Lupoi. Licensing: Annalisa Califano and Beatrice Doti. Editorial Coordinator: Ilaria Tavoni. Art Director: Mario Corticelli. Graphic Design: Marco Paroli. Repro packaging: Mario Da Rin Zanco, Valentina Esposito, Luca Ficarelli, Linda Leporati. Pre-press: Cristina Bedini & Andrea Lusoli. Licensed by Marvel Characters B.V.
This publication may not be sold, except by authorised dealers, and is sold subject to the condition that it shall not be sold or distributed with any part of its cover or markings removed, nor in a mutilated condition. Printed in Italy by Lito Terrazzi . ISBN 978-1-84653-994-7

© 2019 MARVEL

MIX
Paper from
responsible sources
FSC® C115044

MARVEL'S THE AVENGERS PRELUDE 1:
FURY'S BIG WEEK, PART 1

PROLOGUE

1945

OVER THE ARCTIC CIRCLE.

THUMP!

SHINK!

SHUNK!

WHAM!

WHRRRR

WHOOSH!

S.H.I.E.L.D. HQ, NEW YORK
12 HOURS LATER...

DIRECTOR FURY, THANK YOU FOR MAKING TIME IN YOUR BUSY SCHEDULE TO TAKE THIS CALL.

WERE YOU ABLE TO LOCATE THE SUPER-SOLDIER?

DIDN'T LEAVE ME MUCH CHOICE WHEN YOU PULLED THE PLUG ON MY FROSTBITE MISSION.

NO. WE DID LOCATE AN IMPORTANT CLUE THAT COULD HAVE POINTED US IN THE RIGHT DIRECTION, BUT WITH THE EVER-SHIFTING TOPOGRAPHY OF THE GREENLAND ICE SHEET, I IMAGINE WE'LL BE STARTING FROM SCRATCH AGAIN.

A PITY.

YOU WANT TO TELL ME WHAT THIS IS ALL ABOUT?

WE'D LIKE TO HAVE AN OPEN DISCUSSION REGARDING THE PRIMARY OBJECTIVE OF S.H.I.E.L.D. AS AN AGENCY AND OF YOU AS ITS DIRECTOR.

YOU'RE TALKING ABOUT THE TESSERACT.

HEY, NO ARGUMENT HERE. I LOVE THAT OBJECTIVE, IT'S DEFINITELY ONE OF MY TOP THREE OR FOUR FAVORITE OBJECTIVES IN THE WHOLE DAMN HANDBOOK!

BUT AFTER TRYING NUCLEAR, GEOTHERMAL, ELECTRIC, MAGNETIC, ELECTROMAGNETIC, STATIC, KINETIC, SOLAR, AND ABOUT 47 OTHER MIXED VARIANT ENERGY SOURCES WITHOUT ANY RESULTS... WE'RE A LITTLE SHORT ON IDEAS.

REIGNITING THE TESSERACT. THAT IS CORRECT.

THERE IS A WAY, DIRECTOR FURY, BOTH HISTORY AND LEGEND CAN ATTEST TO IT. INSPIRATION WILL STRIKE.

AND WE HOPE TO EXPEDITE THIS PROCESS MOVING FORWARD NOW THAT THE LION'S SHARE OF S.H.I.E.L.D. RESOURCES WILL BE DEDICATED TO THE TESSERACT.

SAY THAT AGAIN?

A PROSPECTUS OUTLINING NEW BUDGETARY ALLOCATIONS WILL ARRIVE SHORTLY. IN KEEPING WITH THE AGENCY'S MANDATE, THE MAJORITY OF FUNDING, EQUIPMENT, AND MANPOWER WILL BE DEDICATED TO ANALYSIS OF THE TESSERACT, CODED AS PROJECT P.E.G.A.S.U.S.

THE PURPOSE OF THIS REDISTRIBUTION IS TO TAKE FOCUS AWAY FROM CURRENT WASTEFUL PROGRAMS AND REDIRECT IT TO P.E.G.A.S.U.S.

WHAT "WASTEFUL PROGRAMS"!?

"IT IS A WASTE OF VALUABLE ASSETS TO PROLONG THE SEARCH FOR STEVE ROGERS, CONSIDERING THAT HIS PURPOSE WOULD BE INSUBSTANTIAL IN THE PRESENT DAY.

"IT IS A WASTE OF PRECIOUS TIME TO CONTINUE CODDLING TONY STARK WHEN ALL YOU NEED CONCERN YOURSELF WITH IS THE ACQUISITION OF HIS WEAPONS TECHNOLOGY.

LET THERE BE ROOOCCCK!!

"IT IS A WASTE OF COUNTLESS PRODUCTIVE MAN HOURS TO MAINTAIN SURVEILLANCE ON DR. BANNER, A MAN THAT HAS LEFT YOU PERPLEXED AND UNDECIDED AS TO ANY COURSE OF ACTION REGARDING HIS EXISTENCE."

WE EMBRACE YOUR ENTHUSIASM, BUT YOUR APPROACH IS MISGUIDED. OUR DECISION IS THAT THE TESSERACT IS OF GREATER SIGNIFICANCE AT THIS POINT IN TIME.

AND IF I CHOOSE NOT TO FOLLOW THESE NEW GUIDELINES SET FORTH IN YOUR "PROSPECTUS"?

THEN YOU'LL BE REPLACED WITH SOMEONE WHO WILL.

IF IT HELPS TO PUT THIS IN PERSPECTIVE, THEN CONSIDER YOURSELF ON NOTICE, DIRECTOR FURY.

THAT TOOK A WHILE.

THEY HAD A LOT TO SAY.

ANYTHING WORTH REPEATING?

NOT IN POLITE COMPANY.

SO... WHAT DO WE DO?

WE KEEP DOING WHAT WE'RE DOING AND TELL THEM THAT WE'RE DOING WHAT THEY WANT US TO BE DOING.

HOW?

HELL, I DUNNO. GET CREATIVE, COOK THE BOOKS. WHATEVER IT TAKES TO LET US DO THIS JOB RIGHT.

...IS THAT THE BEST PLAN OF ACTION MOVING FORWARD?

IF IT'S NOT...

...WE'RE GOING TO FIND OUT THE HARD WAY.

...WHAT A MESS.

NICK FURY
DIRECTOR OF
S.H.I.E.L.D.

FURY'S E

CHAPTE

IG WEEK

R ONE

ONE WEEK EARLIER...

RING! RING!

FURY.

SIR, IN 72 HOURS TONY STARK WILL BE DEAD.

S.H.I.E.L.D. HEADQUARTERS.

DIRECTOR FURY, SENATOR STERN WANTS TO SCHEDULE A SIT-DOWN WITH THE DEPARTMENT OF DEFENSE TO DISCUSS ACQUIRING THE IRON MAN WEAPON.

FIND OUT WHEN HE'S BUSY, AND SCHEDULE IT FOR THEN.

I NEED YOUR SIGNATURE, SIR, FOR THE BUDGETARY REDISTRIBUTION.

SIR, AGENT SITWELL JUST CHECKED IN...

AND?

HE SAID THAT BANNER CLEARED CUSTOMS.

TELL SITWELL TO STAY ON HIM.

SIR, GENERAL ROSS IS ASKING FOR...

TELL HIM NO.

DIRECTOR FURY...

ALL RIGHT, PEOPLE, WHO'S GOT ANSWERS FOR ME?

DIRECTOR FURY, SIR. PLEASE COME WITH ME.

WE DID EXTENSIVE ANALYSIS ON TONY STARK'S SAMPLE--

"--AND DISCOVERED AN UNPRECEDENTED LEVEL OF PALLADIUM RADIOISOTOPES SPREADING THROUGH HIS BLOODSTREAM. YOU'LL SEE THAT HERE..."

OBVIOUSLY THIS IS DIRECTLY RELATED TO THE ARC REACTOR IN HIS CHEST. YOU SEE, PALLADIUM IS A TRICKY ELEMENT.

IT IS SUSCEPTIBLE TO SOMETHING CALLED "CATALYST POISONING" WHERE IT REACTS WITH ANY COMPOUND AND FORMS A CHEMICAL BOND, IN THIS CASE MR. STARK--

YES, I'M SURE IT'S QUITE FASCINATING, BUT IS THERE A CURE FOR IT?

NO.

NO? SIMPLE AS THAT, NO CURE AT ALL?

AS I SAID BEFORE, SIR, IT'S UNPRECEDENTED. AT NO POINT IN HISTORY HAS A HUMAN BEING ENDURED SUCH A PROLONGED AND SELF-INFLICTED EXPOSURE TO PALLADIUM.

EVERY SECOND THAT THE ARC REACTOR REMAINS IN MR. STARK'S CHEST BRINGS HIM CLOSER TO A COMPLETE BREAKDOWN OF THE CIRCULATORY SYSTEM.

AND YOU SAID 72 HOURS?

WELL...THERE IS THIS. LITHIUM DIOXIDE. IT'S NOT A CURE, BUT IT COULD DELAY THE INEVITABLE. STAVE OFF THE SYSTEMS AND GIVE MR. STARK A LITTLE BIT LONGER.

CAN'T YOU MAKE IT STRONGER? PERMANENT?

THERE IS ONE POTENTIAL PROBLEM...

AS AN ELEMENTAL SOLUTION, LITHIUM IS MAKESHIFT AT BEST. NO ELEMENT KNOWN TO EARTH OFFERS A PERMANENT COUNTER-MEASURE TO PALLADIUM.

...IN THEORY, THE LITHIUM DIOXIDE SHOULD SLOW THE SPREAD OF INFECTION, BUT, AS WITH ANY UNTESTED FORMULA, THERE IS THE SLIM CHANCE THAT IT COULD... ⸮AHEM⸮...KILL HIM INSTANTLY.

BZZ! BZZ!

FURY.

STARK'S LOSING CONTROL.

HOW BAD?

I APOLOGIZE... S.H.I.E.L.D. DIRECTOR NICHOLAS FURY... BUT THERE HAS BEEN AN UNFORESEEN DELAY... YOU MUST CONTINUE TO HOLD FOR...FIVE TO TEN MINUTES...

SIR, WE'VE LOCATED TONY STARK.

MARVEL'S THE AVENGERS PRELUDE 2:
FURY'S BIG WEEK, PART 2

TONY STARK'S MANSION.
MALIBU, CALIFORNIA

ENLARGE SCREEN SEVEN.

THAT'S THE THIRD FLARE TODAY.

IT'S WITHIN EARTH'S ATMOSPHERE, SIR.

I SEE THAT. I ALSO SEE THAT EACH INCIDENT HAS RESULTED IN SOME GRAVITATIONAL LENSING.

I KNOW. I'VE NEVER SEEN LENSING THIS SEVERE. IT'S ALMOST AS THOUGH THERE'S SOMETHING TRYING TO PUSH THROUGH THE SPACE-TIME CONTINUUM.

IT IS ALMOST LIKE THAT.

BUT...THAT WOULD BE CRAZY, RIGHT?

INSANE.

MAKE YOURSELF AT HOME, COULSON.

THANK YOU, MR. STARK, I WILL.

AGENT COULSON. VOICE-PRINT VERIFIED.

TRANSFERRING TO DIRECTOR FURY...

I NEED A FACE-TO-FACE.

AGENT ROMANOFF,
A.K.A. BLACK WIDOW.

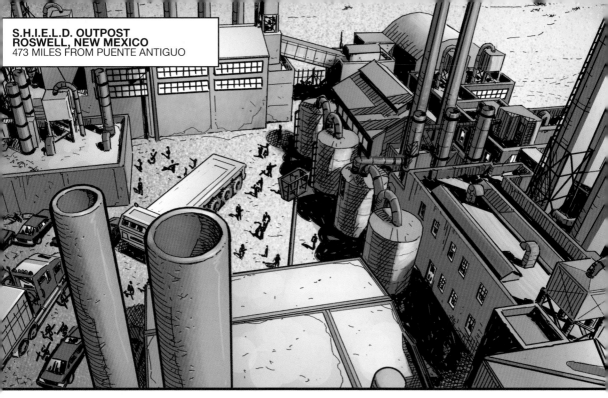

ATTENTION PLEASE! I WOULD LIKE TO THANK ALL OF YOU FOR YOUR PROMPT RESPONSE TIME AND YOUR EFFICIENCY IN PREPARING FOR THIS OPERATION.

OUR TARGET SITE IS ABOUT TWENTY MILES OUTSIDE OF A SMALL TOWN CALLED PUENTE ANTIGUO, THOUGH WE WILL ALSO BE DOING INTEL RECONNAISSANCE WITHIN TOWN LIMITS. WE WILL ALWAYS BE CIVIL AND ONLY EXERT AUTHORITY WHEN ABSOLUTELY NECESSARY.

THERE IS NO WAY TO BE CERTAIN WHAT WE WILL FIND WHEN WE ARRIVE, BUT I AM 100% CONFIDENT THAT THERE IS NOTHING THAT WE CANNOT MANAGE.

ROXXON GAS STATION,
NEW MEXICO

SOMEONE STICK UP THE PLACE?

TRIED TO. LAST NIGHT.

LEMME GUESS: SOME MYSTERIOUS GUYS IN BLACK SUITS BROKE UP THE HEIST?

WHO SAYS WE DON'T LOOK OUT FOR EACH OTHER IN THIS COUNTRY?

COULSON.

BARTON. GLAD YOU COULD MAKE IT.

SO FURY TOLD ME THAT YOU CAUGHT AN ALIEN?

...THEN WHERE'S THE ALIEN THAT IT BELONGS TO?

THAT'S VERY INACCURATE. WE HAVE ENCOUNTERED AN EXTRATERRESTRIAL OBJECT.

HE'S NOT TALKING, IS HE?

NOT YET.

GUY LIKE THAT COULD PROBABLY TAKE MONTHS OF TORTURE BEFORE HE STARTS TO CRACK. IT'S TOO BAD THAT YOU'RE NOT THE TORTURING TYPE.

YOU HAVE AN IDEA, I ASSUME?

YEAH, CUT HIM LOOSE.

LET HIM WALK? JUST LIKE THAT?

AFTER YOU SHACKLED HIM, I SAW SOME CHICK SCRAMBLING BACK TO HER CAR, ALL FRANTIC.

LOGIC SUGGESTS THAT SHE GAVE HIM A RIDE OUT HERE AND SHE WAS ABOUT AS SUBTLE IN GETTING AWAY AS HE WAS IN GETTING IN.

I'M JUST SAYING, HE MAY BE A PRO, BUT THE PEOPLE HE'S MIXED UP WITH DON'T HAVE A CLUE WHAT THEY'RE DOING. YOU WANT INTEL ON THIS GUY? CUT HIM LOOSE AND GIVE HIM A TAIL.

NOT A BAD IDEA.

UNGH!

HEY! EXCUSE ME, WAIT UP!

YOU'RE IN MY PSYCH CLASS.

I THINK YOU'RE MISTAKEN.

NO, I RECOGNIZE YOU. YOU REALLY STAND OUT.

VROOOM VROOOM VROOOM

THAT'S FUNNY. I WAS TRYING TO BLEND IN.

HEY! WHERE YOU GOING?

HE'S LOCKED IN.

PUT TWO CANISTERS IN THERE WITH HIM.

TSSSSSSSSS!

MARVEL'S THE AVENGERS PRELUDE 3:
FURY'S BIG WEEK, PART 3

RRRMMMBBBLLL!

THUD!

CHSS CHSS CHSS!

KOFF! KOFF!

BLONSKY! YOU'RE UP!

WHACK!

DID BANNER DO THIS?

A BUILDING THAT HE KNOCKED OVER, YEAH.

YOU NEED A DOCTOR?

MAYBE A PSYCHIATRIST.

DID GENERAL ROSS GET HIM?

NO, BANNER MADE IT OUT. BUT...

...THEY ENHANCED BLONSKY.

BZZZ! BZZZ!

FURY.

SIR, IT'S COULSON...

THAAAAAAAAT'S NOT NORMAL.

CRACKLE!

GRRRRRUNCH!

BOOM!

SCREEEECH!

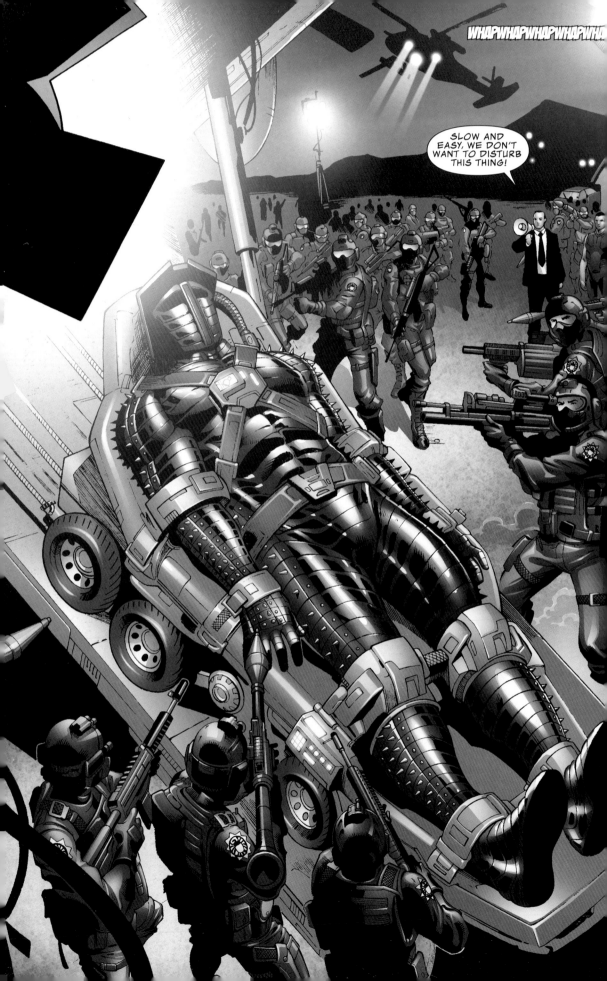

ANDREWS AIR FORCE BASE, MARYLAND.

GENERAL ROSS...

...A WORD?

COLONEL FURY! IN THE FLESH!

AND HERE I THOUGHT YOU'D JUST SEND ONE OF YOUR SNOOPS TO HIDE IN THE SHADOWS AND TAKE NOTES.

I ASSUME THAT YOU HAD THIS THOUGHT WHEN YOU WERE ILLEGALLY BREACHING MY ENCRYPTED DATABASE?

OH NO, YOU'VE GOT IT ALL WRONG. THE WORLD SECURITY COUNCIL GAVE ME CLEARANCE FOR THAT.

I MEAN...YOU DIDN'T REALLY BELIEVE THAT THEY'D TRUST YOU AND YOU ALONE WITH THE SAFETY OF THIS WORLD?

THE WORLD NEEDS BOTH OF US, FURY. I'M OUT ON THE BATTLEFIELD KILLING OUR ENEMIES, AND YOU'RE SAFE BEHIND A WALL PROTECTING ALL THE SECRETS THAT EVERYDAY CITIZENS CAN'T HANDLE.

YOU'RE THE SHIELD, AND I'M THE SWORD.

YOU'RE NOT SHARP ENOUGH TO BE A SWORD, GENERAL.

THAT'S THE OLD ME. THE NEW ME IS EMBRACING THE PRACTICAL APPLICATIONS OF ADVANCED SCIENCE IN MODERN WARFARE. MY TEAM AND I HAVE MADE SOME VERY SIGNIFICANT BREAKTHROUGHS.

I KNOW YOU'D PREFER TO DIG AROUND IN THE ICE FOR ANTIQUATED WEAPONS, BUT I PLACE MORE VALUE IN MOVING FORWARD.

THE "NEW YOU" COULD LEARN A FEW THINGS FROM THE "OLD YOU," ESPECIALLY ON THE SUBJECT OF RUSHING INTO THINGS YOU DON'T FULLY UNDERSTAND.

YOUR HALF-ASSED SUPER-SOLDIER EXPERIMENT IS DANGEROUS, AND I STRONGLY SUGGEST THAT YOU PULL CAPTAIN BLONSKY FROM THE FIELD IMMEDIATELY.

I DON'T TAKE ORDERS FROM YOU, COLONEL.

STAY THE COURSE AND YOU WILL SOON ENOUGH.

WHATEVER HELPS YOU SHUT THAT EYE AT NIGHT. IF YOU'LL EXCUSE ME...

...I HAVE A HULK TO CATCH.

BE-BEEP.

LOCK IN ON MR. GREEN'S LOCATION AND THEN GET THAT INFORMATION TO AGENT ROMANOFF. I NEED HER ON THE MOVE RIGHT AWAY.

"WE NEED TO BRING IN
BANNER, ANYTHING TO
KEEP HIM OUT OF
GENERAL ROSS' PATH."

DIRECTOR FURY,
GENERAL ROSS
BEAT ME HERE.
HE'S TAKEN
BANNER INTO
CUSTODY.

THEY'RE
TAKING HIM
OUT IN A
HELICOPTER, I
WON'T BE
ABLE TO
PURSUE.

OUR INTEL HAD BANNER MEETING
WITH A DR. SAMUEL STERNS. HE'S
A CELLULAR BIOLOGIST, GOT A
LAB ON THE THIRD FLOOR. GO
MAKE SURE THAT BANNER DIDN'T
LEAVE HIM ANYTHING TO
WORK WITH.

COPY
THAT.

RRRMMMMBBBLLL

**MARVEL'S THE AVENGERS PRELUDE 4:
FURY'S BIG WEEK, PART 4**

DR. SAMUEL STERNS?

I THINK PERHAPS ONCE I WAS...

NATASHA ROMANOFF, A.K.A. BLACK WIDOW.

...BUT SHALL NOW BECOME MUCH MORE.

RIGHT, SURE. I'M GOING TO GET YOU MEDICAL ATTENTION.

OH NO, MY DEAR. I AM THE ONLY DOCTOR THAT I WILL REQUIRE. BUT I WILL BE REQUIRING YOUR ASSISTANCE.

MY ASSISTANCE?

FOR I AM CHANGED NOW. I SEE MY FUTURE UNFOLDING. IT IS AN ILLUSTRIOUS FUTURE DEFINED BY POWER AND INFLUENCE. A FUTURE THAT BEGINS THIS VERY INSTANT.

ASSIST ME IN GATHERING MY WORK AND ELUDING THE AUTHORITIES AND THIS EFFULGENT FUTURE WILL BE YOURS ALSO, MY LITTLE RUSSIAN DARLING.

FAINT TRACES OF YOUR ACCENT SUGGEST THAT STALINGRAD WAS YOUR BIRTHPLACE, BUT I SENSE THAT YOU HAVE NOT SEEN A HOME IN MANY YEARS, MY CHILD.

WHATEVER THE EVIL MEN TOOK FROM YOU, WHATEVER YOUR HEART DESIRES, IT WILL BE YOURS. ALL YOU MUST DO FOR ME IS...

NICK FURY
DIRECTOR OF
S.H.I.E.L.D.

DIRECTOR FURY.

AGENT ROMANOFF.

I HEAR THAT BANNER ESCAPED.

YES, BUT GENERAL ROSS TOOK POSSESSION OF THAT OTHER... THING. LOOKED LIKE A DEFORMED DINOSAUR.

THAT'S UNFORTUNATE.

SIR...

...IT'S TOO MUCH. TOO MUCH FOR US TO HANDLE.

NEVER THOUGHT I'D HEAR YOU SAY THAT.

DON'T MISUNDERSTAND ME BECAUSE I FEAR NO MAN... BUT THIS IS DIFFERENT. THESE ARE GODS AND MONSTERS AND MACHINES OF WAR THAT WE'RE MIXED UP WITH.

I'M SUPPOSED TO GO UP AGAINST THE HULK WITH 17 ROUNDS OF ARMOR-PIERCING BULLETS? I DON'T THINK SO.

I DON'T LIKE IT ANY MORE THAN YOU DO, SIR... BUT WE ARE OUTMATCHED. THE SOONER WE ACCEPT IT THE SOONER WE CAN FIX IT... OR THE SOONER WE CAN STOP WASTING OUR TIME PRETENDING THAT WE CAN MAKE A DIFFERENCE.

YOU'RE RIGHT. AND I'D LIKE YOU TO SEE SOMETHING.

PLEASE HOLD FOR THE
LD SECURITY COUNCIL...

LEASE HOLD FOR THE
RLD SECURITY COUNCIL...

DIRECTOR FURY. WE UNDERSTAND THAT YOU HAVE AN IMPORTANT MATTER YOU'D LIKE TO DISCUSS?

YES, I DO.

I'M SENDING YOU A PROSPECTUS FOR S.H.I.E.L.D.'S NEW BUDGETARY ALLOCATIONS.

YOU'LL SEE THAT IT SUBSTANTIALLY INCREASES FUNDING FOR THE AGENCY, EXPANDS JURISDICTION FOR MY AGENTS, AND AUGMENTS MY STRATEGIC AUTHORITY.

CLIK-CLIK-CLIK BLOOP!

YOU ASK FOR QUITE A LOT, DIRECTOR FURY.

THE WHOLE WORLD, SOME MIGHT SAY.

TELL US...HAS THERE BEEN ANY SIGNIFICANT PROGRESS WITH THE TESSERACT RECENTLY?

UMMMM, NOPE.

REIGNITING THE TESSERACT WAS AND WILL REMAIN YOUR PRIMARY OBJECTIVE AS DIRECTOR OF S.H.I.E.L.D. ...

...YET YOU HAVE MADE NO HEADWAY.

PLEASE, ENLIGHTEN US. WHAT HAVE YOU ACCOMPLISHED AS OF LATE THAT WOULD JUSTIFY COMPENSATION OF THIS MAGNITUDE?

HMMM, LET ME THINK...

...IT'S BEEN SUCH A BUSY WEEK.

DIRECTOR FURY...

OH! AND MEANWHILE I'VE KEPT A SMALL TEAM ON THE HUNT FOR STEVE ROGERS, WHICH I KNOW MIGHT BE PERCEIVED AS DISOBEYING ORDERS...

...I JUST THOUGHT IT MIGHT BE HANDY TO HAVE ACCESS TO THE ONLY HUMAN BEING ON THIS PLANET THAT HAS HAD ANY DIRECT EXPERIENCE WITH THE TESSERACT.

ANYWAY, THAT'S WHAT I'VE BEEN UP TO. I'VE ALSO DONE SOME THINKING, AND IN DOING SO I'VE REALIZED THAT...

...THE WORLD IS CHANGING. GETTING MORE DANGEROUS.

ONE THING I KNOW FOR SURE: NOBODY IS BETTER SUITED TO PROTECT THIS WORLD THAN ME AND MY PEOPLE.

ALL WE NEED ARE THE MEANS TO DO WHAT WE DO BEST.

WE HAVE REVIEWED YOUR PROSPECTUS.

YOU WILL HAVE ALL THAT YOU REQUIRE BY MONTH'S END.

BLIP!

EPILOGUE

ONE YEAR LATER...

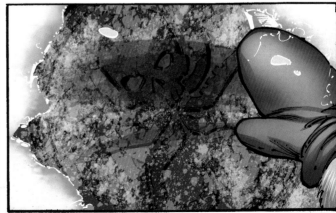

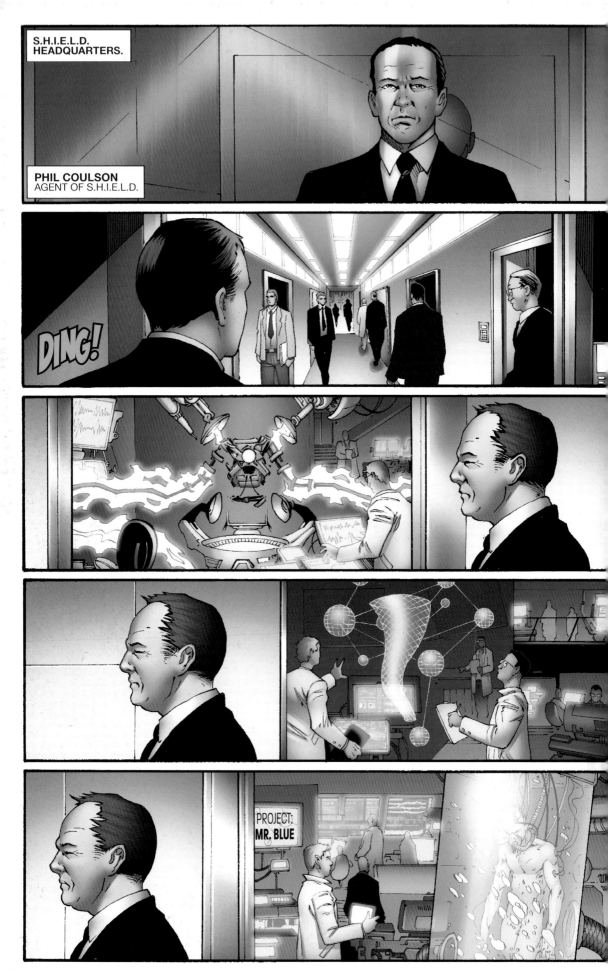

S.H.I.E.L.D.
HEADQUARTERS.

PHIL COULSON
AGENT OF S.H.I.E.L.D.

DING!

PROJECT:
MR. BLUE

THAT'S EXCELLENT WORK, DOCTOR...

THANK YOU, AGENT COULSON.

...NOW I NEED YOU TO DISMANTLE THAT THING, AND MAKE IT ABOUT A HUNDRED TIMES SMALLER.

AND PUT A TRIGGER ON IT!

WASN'T EXPECTING YOU HERE.

I WAS WOKEN UP BY A CALL THIS MORNING...

...A CALL FROM UP NORTH WITH BIG NEWS.

"WE FOUND STEVE ROGERS."

TAKE A DEEP BREATH. I NEED YOU TO GAS UP THE JET AND SET A FLIGHT PATH FOR THESE COORDINATES...

...I JUST HAVE ONE ERRAND TO RUN BEFORE WE TAKE OFF FOR THE ARCTIC.

THE ADVENTURE CONTINUES IN THE MOVIE

COVER-SKETCH BY GERALD PAREL